SUBLIMINAL COMMUNICATION TEST II (SUBCOM-II)

A self-administered, self-scoring test of

- **Subliminal Persuasion**
- **Subliminal Perception**
- **Subliminal Dissuasion**

Charles Edwin Henderson, PhD

Subliminal Communication Test II: (SubcomII)
Charles Edwin Henderson

Published by Alfadore Press, 7613 Elmwood Ave. #620416
Madison, WI 53562-0416

ISBN 978-1-947354-03-6 (Digital Version, PDF format)
ISBN 978-1-947354-02-9 (trade paperback)

**

More about the author:
www.biocentrix.com/charles-e-henderson-phd
www.alfadore.com

IMPORTANT NOTE TO THE READER

PLEASE READ THIS FIRST

Please read the text in the next section, and chapters 1, 2, and 3 before taking the test. The taking of the *Subliminal Communication Test II* was originally designed to be administered by someone trained in how to administer it. That job is now yours. There is not a lot you have to know, but what there is, is important. In fact, without reading the text leading up to the test, you probably would not even know how to take it. Some preparation is required.

Please read the sections before the actual test (no peeking!) so you can take the test correctly the first time. If you do not, you run the risk of introducing extraneous variables that can skew your score in misleading directions. You can easily avoid that by simply reading the instructions in the first three chapters before taking the test.

Be assured the *Subliminal Communication Test II (SubcomII)* is an easy one to take as long as it is done correctly. You can take the test repeatedly if you like. Re-taking of the test typically follows measures taken to improve subliminal communication.

Also, please read initially only up to the test itself. Please do not read the material that follows the test – the *scoring*, *analysis* and *discussion* sections – until *after* you have completed the test the first time.

Subliminal Communication II Test

The *Subliminal Communication II* test (*SubcomII*) is the self-administered, self-scoring version of the original *Subliminal Communication Test* (*Subcom*). The original *Subcom* is a lengthier test. It takes more time and requires computer analysis of the results to derive various factors along a number of dimensions. Such a level of sophistication was desirable and indeed necessary for research purposes.

SubcomII, the test provided here, was derived from the original *Subcom* test and is both easier to take (it does not require another person trained to administer it) and is immensely easier to score. It does not require computerized analysis. It is easily scored using paper and pencil and simple arithmetic.

Please keep in mind that you are filling two roles here, the one who administers the test, and the test taker. It is important that you be diligent in your administration duties so that the test taker – you, probably – can get the most and best information from taking it. It is not complicated but does need to be done correctly.

Complete instructions are included for taking the *SubcomII* test and for scoring it. A chart of comparative results is included to help the test taker evaluate his or her results in terms of how others have done. As already mentioned, it will be better if you do not look at the information following the test until after you have actually taken it. Scores of others who have taken the test, and discussion of various elements, could have an effect on how you score on the test the first time.

The *Analysis and Discussion* section provides further information and will help give insight into the test taker's scores and where improvement is needed. Special emphasis is given to the dimensions of subliminal persuasion.

A more thorough and prescriptive coverage of the topic of subliminal communication, along with training procedures for remediation and improvement, (with special emphasis on subliminal persuasion) can be found in *All-In Selling* (www.allinselling.com) which is available from the publisher, Alfadore Press (www.alfadore.com).

Contents

1

Introduction to the Test

What you can expect from taking this test.
The purpose of the *Subliminal Communication II* test is to provide you with the following kinds of information.

- How well your subliminal communication is functioning.

- Whether you are sabotaging yourself and your efforts – personal as well as career – with negative messages.

- How persuasive or dissuasive your subliminal transmissions to others are.

The *Subliminal Communication Test II* itself cannot tell you how to correct or improve your subliminal communication, but it does give you an indication of what needs work and the direction you need to go in your own remediation efforts. Subliminal dissuasion can be corrected, subliminal perception can be trained to be more sensitive and accurate, and subliminal persuasion can be strengthened and made the norm rather than occasional or haphazard.

Subliminal Transmission.
Subliminal *transmission* is the sending part of subliminal communication. More about this later.

Subliminal Persuasion.
Subliminal *persuasion* is the attempt to positively influence other people's beliefs, attitudes or values. This is the

verb form of *persuasion*, as in *to persuade*. It should not be misconstrued as an argument in the formal or logical sense. Subliminal persuasion is accomplished through subtle, sometimes not so subtle, signs and signals that help support the gist of the message being communicated. Signals that indicate the sender's sincerity and personal conviction are examples of integral components of subliminal communication intended to be persuasive. That is, subliminal persuasion.

Thus to be persuasive one must send subliminal signals that convincingly attest to the speaker's sincerity, integrity, conviction, trustworthiness, and logic, to name just a few.

Subliminal Dissuasion.

To *dissuade* is the opposite of *to persuade*. Dissuasion can be accomplished by sending cues such as untrustworthiness or dishonesty, unsound reasoning, disbelief in the proposition being presented, and so on.

Dissuasion tactics can be engaged by the subconscious mind when the results of a person's attempts to persuade are considered by his or her own subconscious to be undesirable. In other words, the person's subconscious mind is opposed to what he or she is trying to sell or pull off.

Common sense – *conscious* sense, that is – is no help here because the logic of the subconscious mind is entirely different from that of the conscious mind. (For more information see chapter 3, "Minds at Odds," in *All-In Selling*.) (www.allinselling.com.)

Supraliminal Communication.

"Supraliminal" is a term with which you may not be familiar. It is more or less the opposite of subliminal and basically refers to the perception and communication modes that are already familiar to you. Things you know (consciously know) you see, hear, taste, feel and smell are sup*ra*liminal perceptions.

While there is a simple three-letter change (su**B**liminal becomes su**PRA**liminal and vice versa), the difference is significant. *Supraliminal* is sometimes referrred to as *super*liminal. That is a way to keep them straight. Since "limin" means threshold, *super*liminal is above the threshold and *sub*liminal is below it.

Supraliminal perception refers to the processes you know as ordinary seeing, hearing, feeling, smelling and tasting. "Supraliminal transmission" or "cues" are those bits of information others get from you via what they see you doing, hear you saying, and so on.

As you know there can be subtleties of communication in things like facial expression, eye-blink rate, skin flushing (blushing), tone and loudness of voice, arm and hand gesture, body language – the list can get very long.

Some people are better than others at reading people's signs and signals. It varies with age, history, life circumstances, and of course whatever genetic characteristics a person inherits. Genetics can explain a lot of the variation in individual differences, but apparently everyone can improve what they communicate supraliminally. Otherwise there would not be actors' training and the improvement in theatrical performance we can detect as an actor gets more experience and, perhaps, training.

But conscious effort coincidental with experience and training can go only so far. The characteristics of our supraliminal communication are heavily outweighed by subliminal signs and signals. We pay far more attention to what is being subliminally transmitted and perceived which is out of our hands, consciously speaking. It is not possible to consciously control everything.

No more than about 10 percent of our total perception comes from our supraliminal perception. That means that we see, hear, feel, smell and taste nine times more than we are aware of. That is the part of perception we call *subliminal*. The *Subliminal Communication Test II* focuses on this aspect of perception and measures three specific categories: *perception*, *persuasion* and *dissuasion*.

Perception (P_c)

Each sense modality is rich in subliminal cues that are difficult or even impossible to perceive consciously, but that the subconscious can perceive. It is not entirely correct to say that the subconscious mind "perceives" anything since to our knowledge we have only the five senses which provide input to us at both the conscious and the subconscious level. How this division of incoming sensory signals is divided up is not entirely understood at this time but research long ago established that there definitely is perception, the receipt of incoming sensory information, at the subconscious level. We perceive (see, hear, smell, taste and feel) a lot more than we consciously know about.

Consider the human voice as just one way we communicate that is richly laden with subliminal messages. My own research as identified 16 variables – such as tone, frequency changes, and other vocal qualities – that send subliminal cues readily perceived at the subconscious level, but that are difficult to pick up consciously. Even when they are consciously detectable they tend to be consciously ignored by listeners. It is almost certain that there are more such subliminal variables than the 16 I identified.[1]

---

[1]Henderson, Charles E. *Fundamental Frequency of the Human Voice and Personality Traits.* Doctoral dissertation. Order from the United States Library of Contress via ProQuest, UMI Order Number 8121432.

Persuasion (P_s)

You undoubtedly know that "persuasion" means to influence another person or group to think, believe, value, or do what you want them to.

What a lot of people do not know is that our subconscious minds can send out persuasive messages, or cues, that are immensely more potent forms of persuasion. Those subconscious messages can be positive relative to your attempted influence. That is, they are intended to be persuasive.

But the messages (cues, signals, signs) we send out subliminally can also contradict our conscious attempts at persuasion. These are dissuasive messages.

Dissuasion (D_s)

Since subliminal communication is not mind reading it is not possible for the subconscious mind to communicate with another subconscious mind directly with syntactical compositions. If a sentence with a subject and predicate and all that sophomore English stuff is what is meant by "message," then we need to clarify the issue.

One subconscious mind cannot send to another subconscious mind (or several minds if a group or audience is involved) a message like, "This product I am trying to get you to buy is pure crap and a waste of money." To do so would require an immensely complex set of signals with one signal for each element of the sentence. That is not the case and, to my knowledge, never happens.

What we do instead is send what might be called *signals of disconfirmation*. We are consciously privy to some of the more common disconfirmation signals. Like when little Johnny says he did not do it but will not look you in the eye. His shifty-eyedness is a disconfirmation signal which causes you to disbelieve him. His signals are dissuasive.

Consider a slightly more sophisticated example. Emma tells her boss she needs next Wednesday off to take little Johnny to the doctor. Subconsciously she is certain that her arch rival, bitch Olivia, will take advantage of her absence to somehow make trouble for her. So she transmits cues that cause her boss to somehow disbelieve Emma and deny the request.

The fact that this is far more detrimental than any mischief bitch Olivia might have caused is, from the subconscious standpoint, irrelevant. That is because the subconscious mind's logic is entirely different from conscious logic and common sense is virtually useless in trying to understand subconscious motivations.[2]

The same kind of dynamic applies to persuasive messages too, of course. It is just that they are the opposite of dissuasive messages. Persuasive messages or cues are supportive of conscious messages and lend credence to whatever is being said. Or written, for that matter, or even implied with gestures.

Emma's case is one example of why the subconscious might want to sabotage one's efforts with dissuasive messages. Another example is the all-too-common case of a salesperson who has a subconsciously fixed dollar amount of acceptable earnings. The salesperson is consciously unaware of such a limit on income. If the salesperson's limit is about to be exceeded by making a sale, the subconscious is likely to emit dissuasive messages. Bombarded by dissuasive subliminal cues from the salesperson, the prospect unlikely to buy, thereby averting the threat of the salesperson earning too much.

By the way, subconsciously set limits on income are very common. There is good evidence that at least 95 percent of

---

[2]See Henderson, *All-In Selling*, pp. 25-40 www.allinselling.com.

people have some kind of subconsciously imposed limits on how successful they can be.

Fortunately there are reasonably easy procedures for determining and correcting such subconsciously imposed limits (see Henderson, *ibid.*).

2

Definitions

To make sure we are all on the same page, as they say, here are some definitions of terms used in the *Subliminal Communication Test II*.

Message
In subliminal communication parlance, "message" is synonymous with "cue" and "signal." You will understand by now this is not a message in the conventional sense, as in a sentence or language-based message. "Go to the store and bring back a quart of milk" is a sentence or language-based message. This kind of verbal message is not possible with subliminal communication. Instead of verbal composition, the subconscious communicates with signals.

The wagging tail of a dog is a signal. Whether the signal is intentional or not, it is interpreted to have meaning and therefore a sign. We might say that the dog sends a "message" with its tail. This is what is meant by *message* in the parlance of subliminal communication.

Signal, Transmit
"Signal" is the key word here. As a noun it is meant as message. As a verb it refers to the act of transmission. This is the same as to "send." "Radiate" could also be used because subliminal messages are not necessarily *sent* to a specific person or destination. They are rather like

conditions that are present to be read or not read. They exist whether there is anyone reading them or not. Take for example a slight tremolo in one's voice that indicates fear. It requires a perceiver who can discern the tremolo's presence for a message to have been transmitted. If the perceiver does not know what the tremolo means, the only message transmitted is that a tremolo was present. The more the perceiver understands about the meaning or portent of the tremolo, the more "messagy" the signal.

Signal is the word of choice because of the nature of the subconscious mind, its own special logic and concept of reality. "Signal" implies information being "put out there" whether anyone picks up on it (receives and translates it) or not.

Much of the time what is transmitted has been subconsciously generated for the benefit of a particular receiver, or set of receivers. So most of the time the conventional meaning of "transmit" or "send" will suffice, but "signal" is the term used in most of the *Subliminal Communication Test II* questions.

Persuasion

Generally speaking, "persuasion" means to positively influence another person's (or other people's) belief, attitude, value or behavior. Subliminal persuasion is accomplished through manifestly meaningful signals ("messages"). For those who know what it means, the wagging tail of a dog usually signifies friendliness, an absence of aggression or intent to bite. In the same sense, subliminally persuasive messages signify conviction, trustworthiness, sincerity, honesty, authority (especially important), agency (in the sophisticated, psychological sense), social class, relatedness to receivers, and other qualities of similar ilk.

Dissuasion
As you already know, *dissuasion* is the opposite of *persuasion*. Dissuasive subliminals counter conscious messages, as if someone were standing behind you shaking their head "no" while you are saying "yes."

It is important to keep in mind that dissuasive cues are always relative to what you are consciously trying to communicate. Dissuasive cues are the subconscious mind's way of saying, "Don't believe what I am saying." This is achieved by evincing the typical sensory cues of someone who is not trustworthy. Dissuasive cues are especially unfortunate in that they cast a pall of distrust over everything a person subsequently says or does. It takes a long time to win back the trust of someone who has perceived dissuasive signals. (And a subconscious trained to stop sending dissuasive signals.)

Class, status, socioeconomic class
It is politically incorrect in the United States and much of the rest of the Western world to even mention the concept of class. What is meant here is not the kind of class one might be born into, as in the caste system of India.

This is primarily socioeconomic in nature, more perhaps a matter of "prestige." Class differences of this sort always emerge in any human grouping and this is genetically demonstrable. Books have been written on this topic and it is not necessary for us to get into all that here.

To give some specific examples, practicing physicians are in a lower socioeconomic class than surgeons and higher than dentists. (Yes, really!) Dentists are above dental technicians who are higher than bus drivers, and so on. When asked in the test if you do certain things differently depending upon the class of the person, think in terms of this model: would you talk to your doctor the same way you would talk to a homeless person?

Naïf

A *Naïf* is someone who has little or no awareness of subliminal communication and, especially, how it works. Naïfs have not taken significant action to enhance subliminal perception or transmission in any way. In other words, they don't know much about it.

Adept

An *Adept* is a person who is knowledgeable about subliminal communication and has worked toward the specific goals of:

1. enhanced subliminal *perception*;
2. removal or change of subliminal *dissuasion*; and
3. enhanced subliminal *persuasion*.

An *Adept*, then, is someone who has studied subliminal communication or taken courses in it and has worked to improve it.

3

Test Preparation

The *Subliminal Communication Test II* relies on *ideomotion* to get answers from the subconscious part of the mind. Ideomotion is defined as *muscular movement executed under the influence of a dominant idea, being practically automatic and not volitional.* The body moves or changes in some way, prompted by the subconscious, which is beyond conscious control.[1] This is sometimes referred to as *ideomotor behavior*.

There are a number of manifestation of ideomotor behavior. Conditioned reflexes, for example, are a special case of ideomotor behavior. Like blinking your eye when something comes too close to it or salivating when you think about eating a lemon.

The ideomotor behavior used in the *Subliminal Communication Test II* is demonstrated with something called a Chevreul pendulum. Your first task will be to make one.

Tie a piece of ordinary sewing thread or light string to a small washer or ring. The idea is to have a light weight on the end of a 10 or 12 inch length of thread. ("Bob" is what the weight is generally called.) This is your pendulum. What makes it a *Chevreul* pendulum is the way we are going to use it.

Now draw a diagram like the one in figure 3.1 or use the diagram itself if you like. There are six direction of

---

[1]Henderson, *ibid.*, p. 134.

possible swing on the diagram. "Possible swing" means the directions the pendulum can swing when you are holding it.

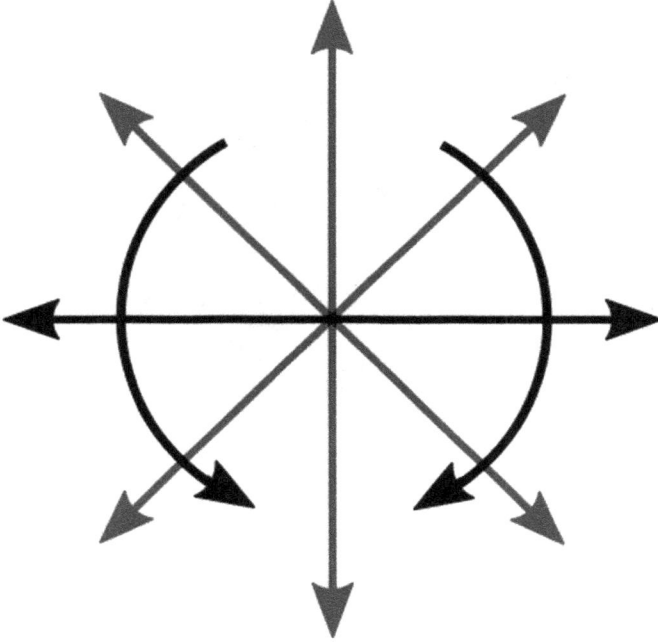

Figure 3.1. *Six potential directions of swing for the Chevreul pendulum.*

Hold the pendulum over the center of the diagram with your elbow resting on the table or desk, or whatever surface you have the diagram on.

Take a look at the pendulum being used in the picture (figure 3.2). This is the way most people ordinarily use the Chevreul pendulum. Use either hand, whichever you prefer. The bob on this pendulum looks like some kind of fancy orb but it is just a common button from an old coat.

The reason there are six directions is because any more than that make it difficult sometimes to determine which direction the pendulum is actually swinging. There is

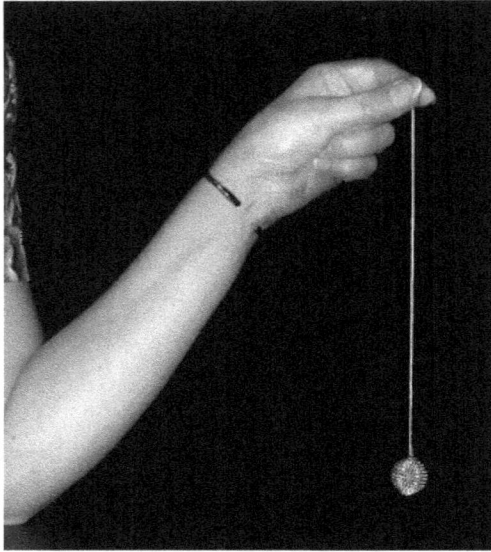

Figure 3.2. Chevreul pendulum in use.

nothing magic about six directions. Six is adequate and keeps the process from getting confusing.

As you hold the pendulum over the diagram pick one of the directions and imagine the pendulum swinging in that direction. Any one of the six will do.

Do not consciously move the pendulum. Just hold it still and wait for it to move on its on. ("On its own" simply means you should not make any conscious effort to get the pendulum to swing. When it moves, you are doing it through ideomotor action or behavior. There is nothing magic, mystical or fiendish about the Chevreul pendulum.)

Once you can get the pendulum to swing in a particular direction just by thinking about it, choose a different direction and get the pendulum to move in that direction.

The *Subliminal Communication Test II* answer mode requires one of five possible answers for each test item. You will get the answer by using the Chevreul pendulum. In other words you want the pendulum (your subconscious mind, actually) to answer each question. There are 40 questions and the answer options to each one look like this:

1. I enjoy taking tests like this.

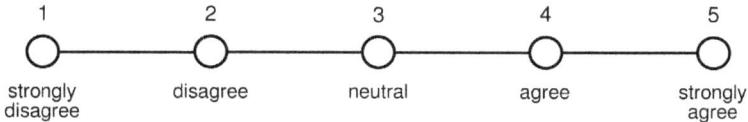

Figure 3.3. Answer options for the Subliminal Communication Test II. Agree-disagree set of answers. Mark or fill-in the circle over the answer that corresponds to the answer given by the Chevreul pendulum.

There are two different answer sets. The agree-disagree set as shown in figure 3.3 and another set as shown in figure 3.4:

2. People put pleasure before profit.

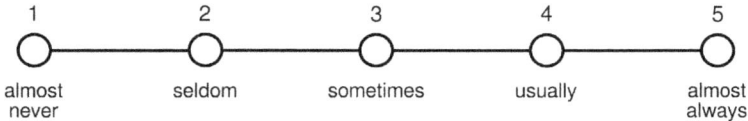

Figure 3.4. Answer options for the Subliminal Communication Test II. Always-never set of answers. Mark or fill-in the circle over the answer that corresponds to the answer given by the Chevreul pendulum.

You will need two answer diagrams fitted with these two sets of answers. Allow yourself to subconsciously select directions of swing to indicate answers. For the first set (*strongly disagree – disagree – neutral – agree – strongly agree*) start with the un-labelled diagram as shown in figure 3.1.

With the pendulum suspended over the center of the diagram, think to yourself that you want a direction of swing that would indicate an answer of "strongly disagree." Wait for the pendulum to swing in a definite direction then mark that direction as the "strongly disagree" answer.

Proceed with this procedure to get the other four answers assigned to different directions. There will be one remaining unassigned direction. Leave it blank as a form of escape hatch for your subconscious.

After you have completed your agree-disagree answer diagram, do the same for the always-never set of answers.

Figure 3.5 gives an example of what you will eventually have on your own diagram. THIS IS JUST AN EXAMPLE. Your subconsciously chosen directions might be entirely different.

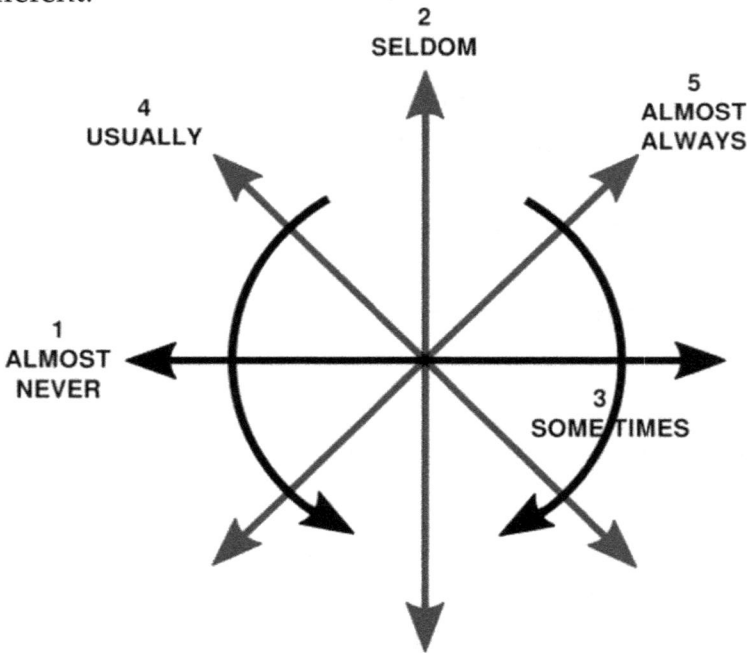

Figure 3.5. Answer options for the Subliminal Communication Test II. Mark or fill-in the circle over the answer that corresponds to the answer given by the Chevreul pendulum.

4

Subliminal Communication Test II

Instructions: Read each numbered statement then allow yourself to respond to it with the Chevereul pendulum held over your answer sheet. Read each statement carefully but do not dwell over-long on it. While waiting for the pendulum to answer – sometimes the answer comes almost immediately, while at other times it may take longer – try to keep your mind as neutral as possible. Once the pendulum is swinging in a definite, discernible direction, mark that answer in the appropriate circle under the statement. Time is not a factor.

TEST

1. I use contradictory subliminal signals to stop myself from getting what I consciously want.

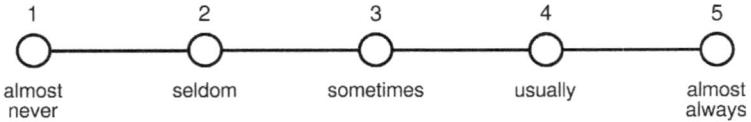

1	2	3	4	5
almost never	seldom	sometimes	usually	almost always

2. I perceive subliminal signals from everyone.

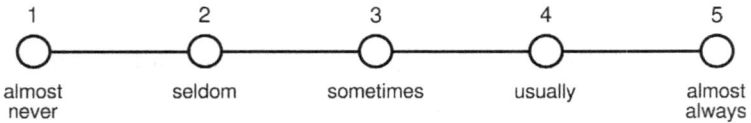

1	2	3	4	5
almost never	seldom	sometimes	usually	almost always

3. I send subliminal signals that agree with what I say.

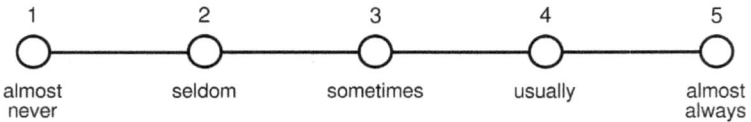

1	2	3	4	5
almost never	seldom	sometimes	usually	almost always

4. Subliminal signals help persuade other people.

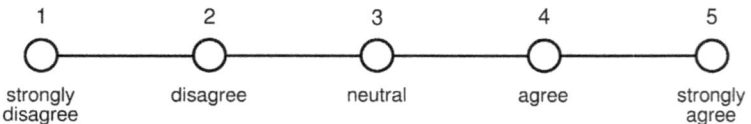

1	2	3	4	5
strongly disagree	disagree	neutral	agree	strongly agree

5. I do not allow myself to earn more than I am worth.

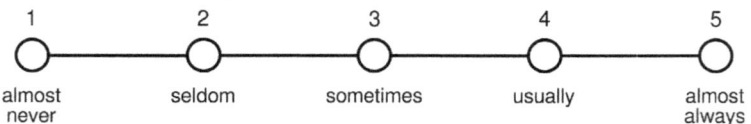

1	2	3	4	5
almost never	seldom	sometimes	usually	almost always

6. I signal persuasive cues to those who make more money than I do.

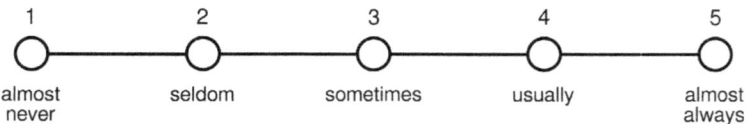

1	2	3	4	5
almost never	seldom	sometimes	usually	almost always

7. Subliminal signals are wasted on the elderly.

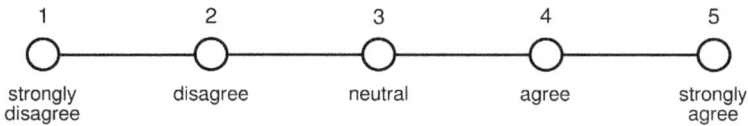

1	2	3	4	5
strongly disagree	disagree	neutral	agree	strongly agree

8. Negative subliminal signals are important to keep from being too successful.

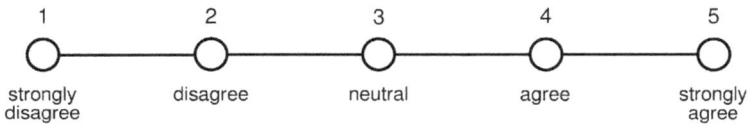

1	2	3	4	5
strongly disagree	disagree	neutral	agree	strongly agree

9. I signal subliminally persuasive messages.

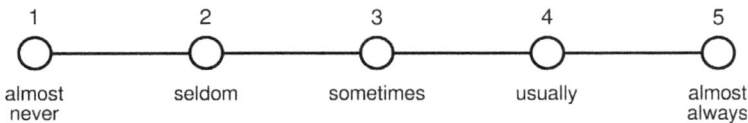

1	2	3	4	5
almost never	seldom	sometimes	usually	almost always

10. Persuasive subliminal cues influence people of the opposite sex.

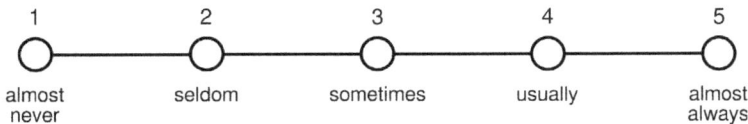

1	2	3	4	5
almost never	seldom	sometimes	usually	almost always

11. I sense things about other people that I am consciously unaware of.

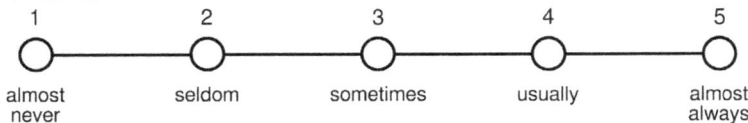

1	2	3	4	5
almost never	seldom	sometimes	usually	almost always

12. My subliminal signals agree with what I am saying.

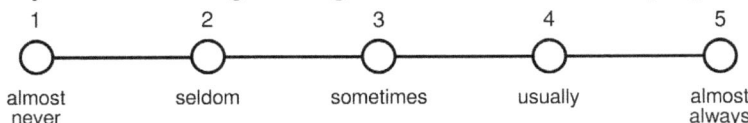

1	2	3	4	5
almost never	seldom	sometimes	usually	almost always

13. I signal negative cues to people of the opposite sex.

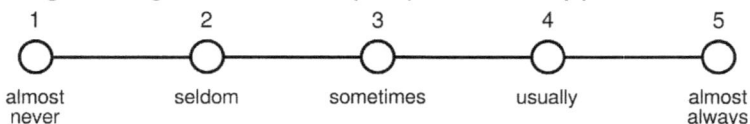

1	2	3	4	5
almost never	seldom	sometimes	usually	almost always

14. I signal negative subliminal cues to avoid too much responsibility.

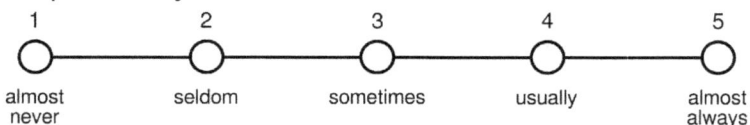

1	2	3	4	5
almost never	seldom	sometimes	usually	almost always

15. I know what people of the opposite sex are thinking.

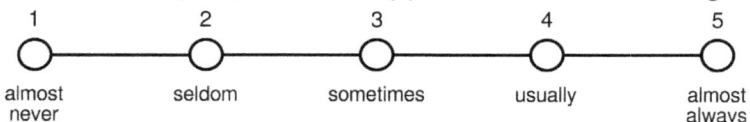

1	2	3	4	5
almost never	seldom	sometimes	usually	almost always

16. Contradictory subliminal cues maintain individuality.

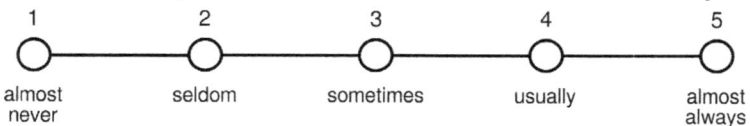

1	2	3	4	5
almost never	seldom	sometimes	usually	almost always

17. I can tell when a person is lying.

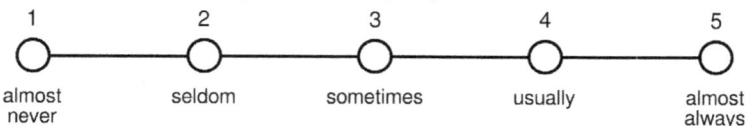

1	2	3	4	5
almost never	seldom	sometimes	usually	almost always

18. I adjust my subliminal signals according to the subliminal signals from others.

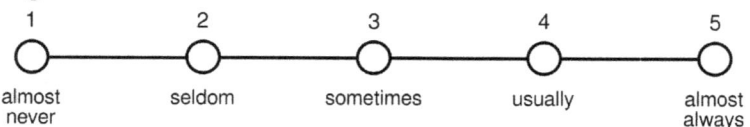

1	2	3	4	5
almost never	seldom	sometimes	usually	almost always

19. Elderly people do not send out subliminal signals.

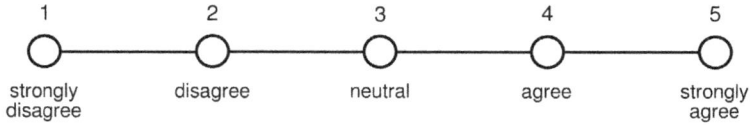

1	2	3	4	5
strongly disagree	disagree	neutral	agree	strongly agree

20. I purposely confuse subliminal signals to people I don't like.

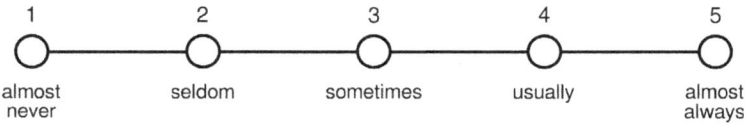

1	2	3	4	5
almost never	seldom	sometimes	usually	almost always

21. I signal persuasive subliminal cues to people with authority over me.

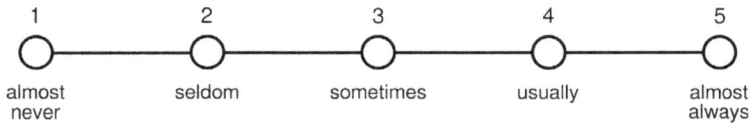

1	2	3	4	5
almost never	seldom	sometimes	usually	almost always

22. I show subliminal signals to people beneath my status.

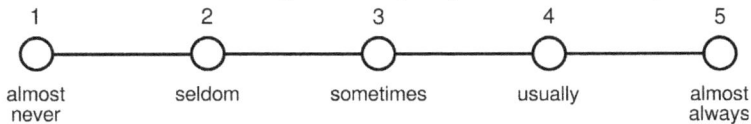

1	2	3	4	5
almost never	seldom	sometimes	usually	almost always

23. I ignore subliminal signals from people I dislike.

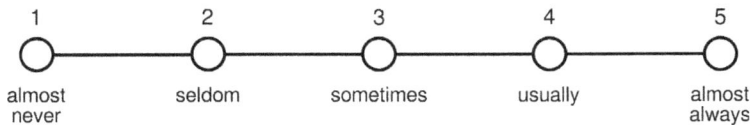

1	2	3	4	5
almost never	seldom	sometimes	usually	almost always

24. Persuasive subliminal signals do not influence other people.

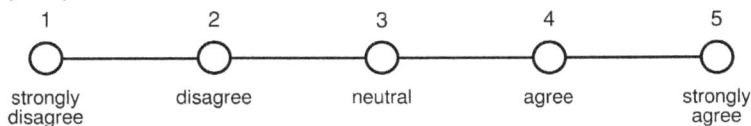

1	2	3	4	5
strongly disagree	disagree	neutral	agree	strongly agree

25. It is best to avoid subliminal signals to people I don't trust.

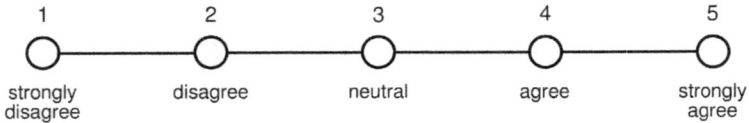

1	2	3	4	5
strongly disagree	disagree	neutral	agree	strongly agree

26. I use dissuasive subliminal signals to avoid emotional closeness.

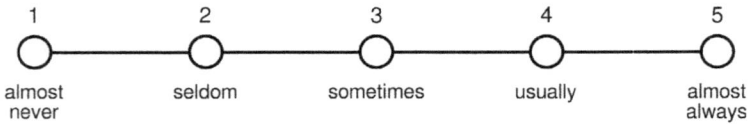

1	2	3	4	5
almost never	seldom	sometimes	usually	almost always

27. People with higher social status signal fewer subliminal cues.

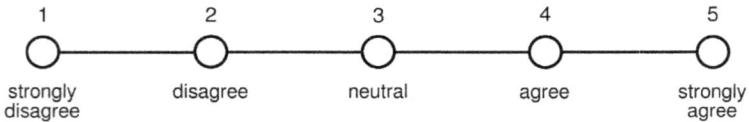

1	2	3	4	5
strongly disagree	disagree	neutral	agree	strongly agree

28. I use subliminal cues to persuade others to agree with me.

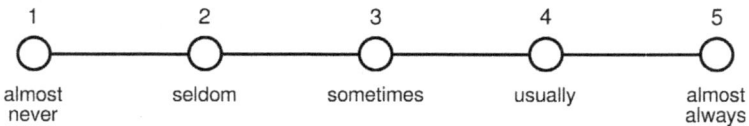

1	2	3	4	5
almost never	seldom	sometimes	usually	almost always

29. I perceive dissuasive subliminal signals just as well as I perceive positive signals.

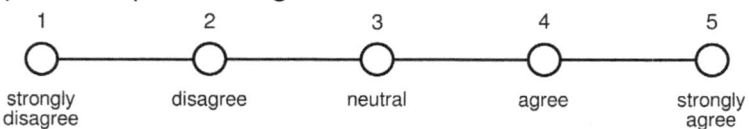

1	2	3	4	5
strongly disagree	disagree	neutral	agree	strongly agree

30. I signal persuasive subliminal cues to get agreement from others.

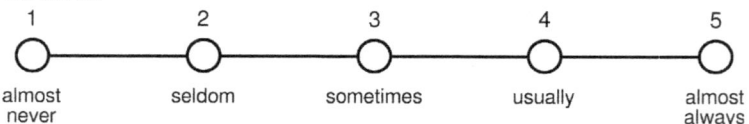

1	2	3	4	5
almost never	seldom	sometimes	usually	almost always

31. I perceive subliminal signals regardless of people's age.

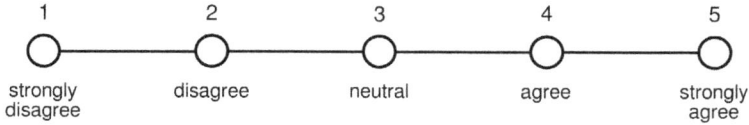

1	2	3	4	5
strongly disagree	disagree	neutral	agree	strongly agree

32. Children respond to my subliminal signals.

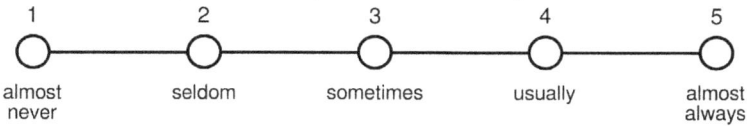

1	2	3	4	5
almost never	seldom	sometimes	usually	almost always

33. I have trouble reading the subliminal cues of people of the opposite sex.

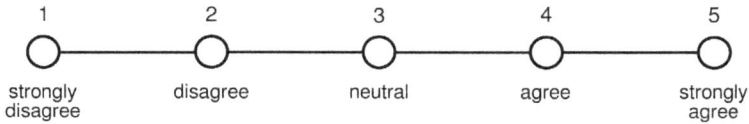

1	2	3	4	5
strongly disagree	disagree	neutral	agree	strongly agree

34. I know which people to trust.

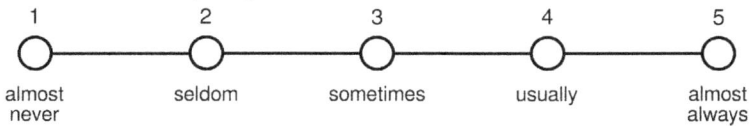

1	2	3	4	5
almost never	seldom	sometimes	usually	almost always

35. I use subliminal signals to let people know what I really think.

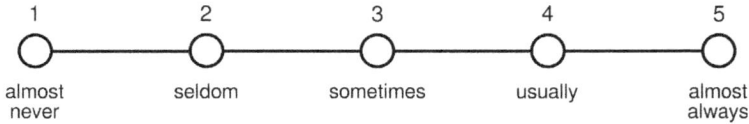

1	2	3	4	5
almost never	seldom	sometimes	usually	almost always

36. I win at card games.

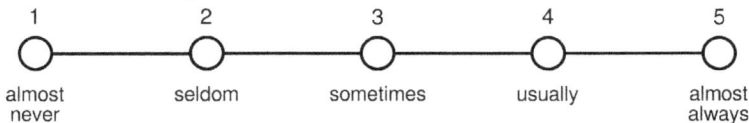

1	2	3	4	5
almost never	seldom	sometimes	usually	almost always

37. Subliminal signals are too dangerous to use.

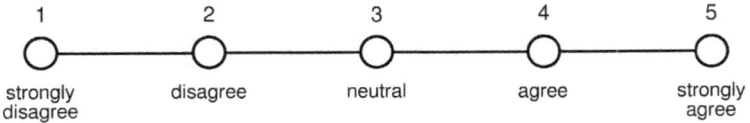

1	2	3	4	5
strongly disagree	disagree	neutral	agree	strongly agree

38. Other people's subliminal signals influence how I feel about them.

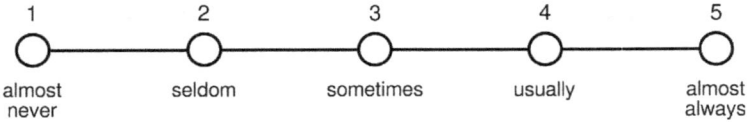

1	2	3	4	5
almost never	seldom	sometimes	usually	almost always

39. I know how to be persuasive with subliminal signals.

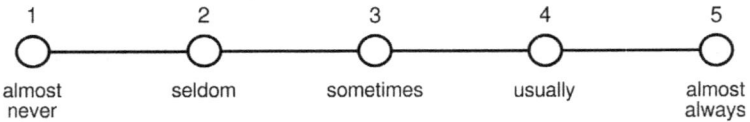

1	2	3	4	5
almost never	seldom	sometimes	usually	almost always

40. Subliminal signals are a good way to avoid undesirable levels of success.

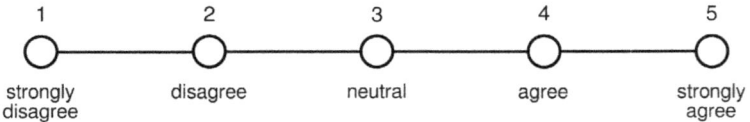

1	2	3	4	5
strongly disagree	disagree	neutral	agree	strongly agree

END OF TEST

Review your test answers to make certain *all* questions have been answered with one of the five given options.

To score your results continue to the next chapter.

5

Scoring the *Subliminal Communication Test II*

Enter your rating number for each item in the designated place on the scoring sheet below. Then sum the three columns for your cumulative score.

For those items with **6-MINUS-RATING** below the item number, subtract your rating (*1* through *5*) from 6 and enter the result in the box. For example, if you rated an item *2* and that is one with the **6-MINUS-RATING** beneath the item number on the scoring sheet, subtract your ranking (*2*, in this example) from **6** and put the result, *4*, in the scoring box. Only certain items are marked for this treatment.

Place your score in the clear box (not in either of the grayed-out boxes). Please note that the scores of three items (18, 36 and 37) are entered in two categories.

When all 40 items have been scored, add the scores in each column on each page and enter the sums in the SUBTOTAL spaces on each page. Then add all the subtotals and put the sums in the indicated spaces at the end of the test.

Question 17 is a special case and is not to be entered for calculation of your score. Ask the question, and record your answer where you can get to it later. This item will receive special treatment in the analysis of your results.

SCORING

QUESTION NUMBER	PERCEPTION P_C	PERSUASION P_S	DISSUASION D_S
1			
2			
3			
4			
5			
6			
7 6-MINUS-RATING			
8			
9			
10			
11			
12			
13			
14			
SUBTOTAL			

QUESTION NUMBER	PERCEPTION P_C	PERSUASION P_S	DISSUASION D_S
15			
16			
* 17 *			
18			
19 6-MINUS-RATING			
20			
21			
22			
23 6-MINUS-RATING			
24 6-MINUS-RATING			
25 6-MINUS-RATING			
26			
27 6-MINUS-RATING			
28			
SUBTOTAL			

QUESTION NUMBER	PERCEPTION P_C	PERSUASION P_S	DISSUASION D_S
29			
30			
31			
32			
33 6-MINUS-RATING			
34			
35 6-MINUS-RATING			
36			
37 6-MINUS-RATING			
38			
39			
40			
SUB-TOTAL			
TOTAL			

6

Analysis and Discussion

In the **Perception** P_C **Comparative Data** table you can see the average scores on each item of a large number of Naifs and Adepts. The scores of an examplar – one of the highest paid, most successful salespeople to ever take the *SubcomII* test – are also included.

Insert your score by each question number under YOUR SCORE, then add your scores and divide by 15 to get your mean (average) score. (See the formula for this following the table.)

Perception P_C Comparative Data

QUESTION NUMBER	YOUR SCORE	P_C NAÏF	P_C ADEPT	P_C EXEMPLAR
2		1.92	3.5	4
11		3.01	4.38	4
15		2.97	3.84	4
18		1.93	2.99	5
19		4	1.97	3
23		1.59	4.03	5

QUESTION NUMBER	YOUR SCORE	P_C NAÏF	P_C ADEPT	P_C EXEMPLAR
27		2.01	3.9	4
29		3.27	3.79	5
31		1.87	3.76	3
33		2.03	3.72	4
34		1.99	4.43	5
36		2.79	3.52	4
37		1.93	4.3	5
38		2.07	3.96	4
39		2.87	4.08	5
MEAN		2.42	3.74	4.27

To get your mean score, add up your answers and divide that sum by 15:

$$\frac{Score\ Total}{Number\ of\ Items\ (15)} = \text{MEAN } P_C$$

It is worth taking the time to compare your scores with those of others on each item. Take the time to reflect on the nature of the question and you will undoubtedly come up with further insight into how you communicate subliminally and in which directions you need to improve.

There are probably numerous approaches to improving subliminal communication, especially along the persuasion dimension, but the only one I know to work is the method I describe and include instructions for in *All-In Selling* (www.allinselling.com).

*   *   *

In the **Persuasion P_S Comparative Data** table you will see the cumulative scores for the subliminal persuasion items. Follow the same procedure you used in the Perception table to add your scores on the Persuasion items, then sum them and divide by 19 to get your mean Persuasion score. (See the formula for this simple arithmetic operation following the **Persuasion P_S Comparative Data** table.)

Persuasion P_S Comparative Data

QUESTION NUMBER	YOUR SCORE	P_S NAÏF	P_S ADEPT	P_S EXEMPLAR
3		1.93	3.39	4
4		2.77	4.07	5
6		1.89	3.56	3
7		3.91	4.59	5
9		3.42	4.16	5
10		3.01	4.6	4
12		2.66	4.31	5
18		3.77	4.86	5

QUESTION NUMBER	YOUR SCORE	P_S NAÏF	P_S ADEPT	P_S EXEMPLAR
21		2.57	4.11	5
22		2.14	4.66	5
24		2.15	4.28	5
25		1.73	4.07	5
28		2.31	4.48	5
30		1.74	4.09	4
32		2.37	3.95	4
35		2.03	4.55	5
36		3.03	4.26	5
37		1.77	4.68	4
39		1.66	3.82	4
MEAN		2.47	4.24	4.58

To get your mean score, add up your answers and divide by 19:

$$\frac{Score\ Total}{Number\ of\ Items\ (19)} = \text{MEAN } P_S$$

*   *   *

In the **Dissuasion** D_S **Comparative Data** table you will see the cumulative scores for the subliminal dissuasion items. This dimension is scored in the opposite direction of the other two. That is, whereas higher scores are preferable in both Perception and Persuasion, a *lower* score is preferable on the Dissuasion part of the test.

Follow the same procedure you used in the above two cases. Enter your Dissuasion scores by their respective item number in the column for your scores, then add up your answers and divide the sum by 9 to get your mean Dissuasion score.

Dissuasion D_S Comparative Data

QUESTION NUMBER	YOUR SCORE	D_S NAÏF	D_S ADEPT	D_S EXEMPLAR
1		3.96	1.87	2
5		4.68	2.39	2
8		3.91	1.87	2
13		4.09	2.88	2
14		4.49	1.77	1
16		3.87	2.56	3
20		3.72	3.09	2
26		4.38	1.97	2
40		4.37	2.23	1
MEAN		4.16	2.29	1.89

To get your mean score, add up your answers and divide by the total number of Dissuasion items (9):

$$\frac{Score\ Total}{Number\ of\ Items\ (9)} = \text{MEAN } D_S$$

It is important to remember that the Dissuasion items are ranked in the opposite direction of Perception and Persuasion scores. Whereas a higher score in either Perception and Persuasion is better, a *lower* score on Dissuasion is better. You can of course reverse this valence by subtracting all the Dissuasion scores and means from 5 to reverse the polarity and make a *higher* score better than a *lower* score. You will probably not find that necessary to conceptually deal with the scores. Just remember that higher is better on the two P dimensions and lower is better on the D dimension.

In general, dissuasion takes place when you are subconsciously opposed to what you are consciously trying to do. You can probably imagine numerous ways this could come about in your life. Here are what we have found to be the most common (and usually disturbing) sources of dissuasive subliminal communication:

- **Moral turpitude.** The subconscious mind is the seat of internalized values inherited or inculcated during childhood. Sometimes these values can be screwy because of the subconscious mind's limited logic. If you are in some way about to violate subconscious moral values you may very well trigger dissuasive subliminal cues to thwart your efforts.

- **Personal worth.** Research and practical experience indicate that at least 95 percent, and perhaps as much as 99 percent of the human population have subconscious limits on how much they believe they are worth. This usually plays out in financial earnings.

If you are about to earn more than you subconsciously think you should, dissuasive subliminal cues are one of the subconscious mind's ways of preventing that from happening.

- **Personal harm.** This one is self-explanatory since one of the primary functions of the subconscious is to keep a person out of trouble. Obviously it only works part of the time and with some people, undoubtedly limited by its own form of logic.

There are other situations and circumstances that can trigger dissuasion but moral turpitude, personal worth and personal harm are three of the more common ones.

*   *   *

You may have noticed that in each of the dimensions the exemplar's scores were not perfect. Some are even surprising in that you might expect that someone who is such an accomplished subliminal communicator, with great skills of persuasion, would be close to if not absolutely perfect. The exemplar's scores are good news for the rest of us because they illustrate how perfection is not required. They also indicate that even slight improvement can make a very large difference in communicative performance. This is exactly what we have found in practice and it applies especially to subliminal persuasion.

so even a slight improvement in subliminal persuasion, in conjunction with the reduction or removal or subconsciously imposed limits to success, can make a very large difference in one's life.

For Perception (P_C) and Persuasion (P_S), the individual rankings for each item, and their combined averages, are all adjusted to range from bad (1) to good (5). Some of the items have reversed polarity, so to speak, which is why they require subtraction from 6 to keep them going in the same direction.

Test Item 17

It is amazing how many people are absolutely certain they can tell when someone is lying.   Yet all kinds of sophisticated research has amply demonstrated that no one is capable of reliably detecting fabrication by another person.

It is true that some people are such poor liars that most people – though not everyone – can tell when they are not telling the truth.

On the other hand some people are so good at lying hardly anyone can catch them at it.

This much you already know. But what you might not know is this: the subconscious mind, which is the source of the answers to the *Subliminal Communication Test II*, does not distinguish between truth and untruth.

Please take note of the cagey choice of words here. An untruth is not necessarily the same as a lie. We consider a lie to be a fabrication in opposition to what is consciously known to be true. If you make a statement that you believe to be true, but it proves later to be untrue, you are not said to have lied. You were merely wrong.

On the other hand if you know you are saying something that is not true, you are lying.

Again, this much you probably already know, at least you do if you have given the matter any thought. But what you are reasoning with is conscious logic. Subconscious logic is quite different. Consciously you function with both deductive and inductive logic. Subconsciously you use only deductive logic.[1]

---

[1] This is not the place to get into the details of subconscious logic. I refer you to the book *All-In Selling* which I have already mentioned.

Consider item 17 from the test: "I can tell when a person is lying." Experience has demonstrated that answers (from the subconscious, remember) can vary all over the map. Following are some of the basic considerations and indications from possible answers.

1. ALMOST NEVER. First, take a look at your P_C score because there can be an interrelationship between falsehood detection and subliminal perception. If your mean P_C score is low the conjunction between it and this rating probably indicates you need an overall improvement in your subliminal perception. If your P_C score is 3 or higher this could indicate either a realistic appraisal of lie-detection capability or just that your subconscious is relatively disinterested in the subject, which would make sense considering how unreliable lie-detection of any sort is.

2. SELDOM. There may not be much difference between a 2 and a 1 on item 17. In fact you will discover, if you take the test (or ask certain questions) more than once that you can get varying answers from one time to the next. A slightly more accurate picture of your subliminal communication emerges after you have taken the test five times and averaged your average scores. But five times? Most people are not that motivated. At least not in the short term.

3. SOMETIMES. This should be the most accurate answer, especially if your P_C score average is 3 or higher. Most people can "sometimes" tell when *some* people are lying. Here is a second level test you can try: establish YES and NO directions of swing with the pendulum and then ask this question:

"Are there some people that I can never tell if they are lying?"

4 or 5. USUALLY or ALMOST ALWAYS. These are unrealistic answers and can indicate a couple of things. One is simply "first-session syndrome" and if that is what it is you will get more realistic answers upon repeating question 17.

This can also indicate poor subliminal perception on one hand, or on the other, poor subconscious interpretation of subliminal perceptions. Both can be improved with training.

*   *   *

As you can probably imagine, an almost infinite amount of discussion could be focused on the 40 items of the test. But each one is sufficiently simple it should not be hard to glean further meaning beyond just the simple ratings about yourself and the implications for your subliminal communication.

There are a few of the test items I wish had been worded differently. But changing them now would mean discarding all the previous data and starting all over again, especially concerning such matters as internal consistency and reliability of several types. So the questions remain the same and, even though some are awkwardly worded, they work.

There are of course no right or wrong answers to the test, just "better" or "not so good." Most people find it helpful to more or less calibrate where they are in their lives with their scores. If things are going along well in life and you have middle of the road scores, you might be satisfied to leave it at that.

But if you are not happy with your personal, social, or career success at this point in your life, and your subliminal communication scores are not particularly good, you have a good idea of the problem and what needs improving.

For more information and coverage of this topic please see *All-In Selling* (www.allinselling.com).

www.ingramcontent.com/pod-product-compliance
Lightning Source LLC
Chambersburg PA
CBHW060632030426
42337CB00018B/3325